Unless otherwise indicated, all Scripture quotations are taken from the Amplified Version of the Bible.

NURTURING A GRACEFUL HEART
Copyright © 2014 by Beverly Jones-Durr
Published by: Gifted Genie Publishing
Madison, Alabama 35757
ISBN 978-0-9897187-1-4
Library of Congress Cataloging –in-Publication Data has been applied for.

All Rights Reserved. No part of this publication may be reproduced, stored in a retrieval system, or otherwise transmitted in any form or by any means—electronic, mechanical or digital, photocopy, recording or any other—except for brief quotations in printed reviews, without the prior permission of the author.

Printed in the United States of America

Dedication

I would like to dedicate Nurturing a Grateful Heart to my family and friends who have prayed for me, encouraged me, challenged me and supported me throughout my journey. Through our relationships, I have learned so much about love and life and what truly matters to me. To my husband, Harry, I thank you for giving me the gift of having you in my life.

CONTENTS

The Basics……………………………………….7

It Started with a Dream…………………..11

The Benefits…………………………………..15

Situations and Events…………………….19

The Seed……………………………………..22

Excavation…………………………………..27

More Than a Feeling…………………….35

Fine Tuning Your Circuitry………………39

Time to Get Real……………………………43

Contents

You Got Stuff..**47**

Who Took My Gratitude? **52**

Tool Box (Gratitude Journal) **55**

Tool Box (Gratitude Letter) **59**

Tool Box (Gratitude Living) **62**

The Village People **65**

Wisdom **69**

It's All About Actions **72**

The Heart **76**

Life Flows **80**

Creating Your Gratitude List **84**

Also written by Beverly Jones-Durr

21 Day Gratitude Challenge

NURTURING A GRATEFUL HEART

THE BASICS

Everything starts someplace. The universe itself was created out of nothing. (Gen 1:1) In order to understand anything, one must start with the basics. This is especially true when it comes to gratitude. According to Merriam-Webster dictionary, gratitude is defined as a feeling of appreciation or thanks. But for me, that definition although accurate only touches the surface of the enormity of the word. Gratitude is also an acknowledgement of a benefit that you have either received or expect to receive. There's a definite relationship between gratitude and spirituality. They are not dependent on the other, but it is generally thought that one who is deeply spiritual understands the benefits of gratitude. The Christian faith views gratitude as a virtue because it not only has the power to shape emotions and thoughts, but actions and deeds as well. Martin Luther considered gratitude as "The Basic Christian Attitude" and still today it is referred to as the "heart of the gospel".

There are also psychological conversations and findings about gratitude. Since it has been recognized that gratitude appears to be a strong determinant of people's well-being, several psychological interventions have been developed to increase gratitude. A group of psychologist had subjects to participate in several different gratitude exercises, such as thinking about a living person for whom they are grateful, writing about someone for whom they are grateful, and writing a letter to deliver to someone for whom they are grateful. The subjects in the control condition were asked to describe their living room. Subjects who engaged in a gratitude exercise showed increases in their experiences of positive emotion immediately after the exercise, and this effect was strongest for those who were asked to think about a person for whom they are grateful. Those subjects who had grateful personalities to begin with showed the greatest benefit from these gratitude exercises. In another study concerning gratitude, participants were randomly assigned to one of six therapeutic behavioral conditions designed to improve the participants' overall quality of life. Out of these conditions, it was found that the biggest short-term effects came from a "gratitude visit" where participants wrote and delivered a letter of gratitude to someone in their life. This condition showed a rise in happiness scores by 10 percent and a significant fall in depression scores, results which lasted up to one month after the visit. Out of the six conditions, the longest lasting effects were associated with the act of writing gratitude journals where participants were asked to write down three things they were grateful for every day. These participants' happiness scores also increased and continued increasing each time they were tested over time after the experiment. However, the greatest benefits were usually found to occur around six months after treatment began. This exercise was so successful that although participants were only asked to continue the journal for a week, many participants continued to keep the journal long after the study was over.

So, you have a general idea of the basics of gratitude, but are you beginning to ask yourself, "What now?" Don't worry…its coming.

It Started with a Dream

You may not know this about me, but I get my best guidance in my dreams. For as long as I can recall, my dreams have been unusual. I don't mean that in a crazy twilight zone kind of way, but rather an informative guiding manner that always led me to the next thing. I have had countless next things in my life in which I followed through on the guidance and information I received. However, there have also been times when I pretended the dream didn't really happen or that I didn't understand the guidance I was given. I am NOT a psychic or a medium, but I am a person whose relationship with God is such that from time to time He guides me to my next thing. So, one night after falling to sleep I dreamed I was sitting in a garden beside a small pond. The glow from the moon reflected off the pond. The air was fresh and for some reason, I could smell the faint scent of Lavender. I was alone in the garden, but I felt the warm closeness of love around me. I was calm, relaxed and unafraid. It was then that I heard His words. The sound of the Fathers voice is one that once heard you never forget. He called me "daughter" and I answered, "Yes, Father". I heard Him whisper the word "Gratitude". The word seemed to float across the pond just above the illumination of the moon. I could see the word – G-R-A-T-I-U-D-E as it floated like a feather above the pond. As it approached me, I held out my hand and like a feather the word landed in my palm. I could feel compassion, love, thankfulness and power. When I awakened, the palm of my hand was slightly red…as if the blood increased its pulsing while I slept. I can't describe the feeling I had at that moment sitting in the bed. But I knew from my past dreams in which I had heard the voice of God…this was my next thing! I took out my journal I kept on the table beside the bed and begin to write. I started with the dream as I remembered it vividly. I had questions in my mind and as quickly as they appeared so did the answer. It was like having a conversation in writing. You're probably wondering if I ever sleep. Yes, I sleep very well when I acknowledge my dream and write about it in my journal. I have learned from experience that when God has a message to give you…He will not be ignored! At any rate, I finished writing all I felt compelled to write and went back to sleep. Did I remember the next morning what had happened? Always! I got my cup of coffee, sat down and read my last journal entry. It was amazing. God wanted me to write about gratitude in a way that His children would understand the power of the gift we have received. That's right! We have all been given the gift of gratitude, but some of us don't know how powerful it can be. If you follow along with me I promise you will have a new perspective if not a stronger one of the power of gratitude. I opened my mind and heart in search of this amazing gift that God had given. It took me to my very core, a place deep inside of my heart where the seed of gratitude was planted. Yours is also planted deep inside your heart. Like any seed, it needs something to ignite it, to grow to its full potential. Now, this gratitude thing is not a task you check off of a list of things to do. It is a process. If you know anything about processes…they take time. The benefits of locating your gratitude seed are enormous. Gratitude fully activated and functional flowing from your core is challenging to achieve but not impossible. There is work to be done. Why should you do the work? I hear you asking. Let me share this poem with you I found on the internet about a grateful heart. The author isn't known. Remember, that gratitude seed is sitting in your heart deep within your core. We are going to work on that.

A Grateful Heart
A grateful heart is one who's lived
Through trials along the way…
Then found the strength to look ahead
And face another day.

A grateful heart is one who knows
That sorrow does not last…
And morning brings a ray of hope
To chase away the past.

A grateful heart will always be
Much stronger than the rest…
For it have weathered every storm
And conquered every test.

The Benefits

When I was a little girl growing up in Birmingham Alabama, my mother assigned chores for me and my sisters to do on a daily basis. We were typical kids…not wanting to do anything but have fun. Sometimes, we would rush through our chores just to go play with our friends. Rushing usually meant half doing the job. Sometimes mom would notice our sloppy work before we even got to the front porch. I remember once we made it all the way to the playground. All our friends were there. It was a beautiful day and we were swinging on the swings screaming like kids having fun do. All of a sudden my swing came to a complete stop! My mom had driven to the playground and she looked pretty angry. I had an idea why. She had discovered that instead of folding my clothes and putting them away, I had tossed them in the closet and closed the door. In my haste to play with my friends I had neglected to completely close the closet door. My punishment was to sit in my room on that beautiful sunny day while the rest of the family had a barbeque on the lawn. All my friends and their families were invited. Looking back, I realize that the punishment was just. I also have discovered that there were benefits in doing the job correctly each time. I had rushed through my chores so many times before that it became an automatic don't think about it moment. I am sure I disappointed my mother by doing so, but patiently she waited for an opportunity to teach me a much deserved lesson. I am grateful for that lesson because not only have I never forgotten it but it changed my perception of responsibility. In life, there are countless opportunities that place us in position to acknowledge and embrace gratitude. I am sure that sitting on that bed in my room hearing all the fun outside my window, I was not thinking about gratitude. I was probably angry at my mother for grounding me. What can I say? Children sometimes miss the point. However, if you repeat the situation enough times you figure it out. Even though I was miserable sitting there, I have to admit I knew it was my fault. I should have done a better job simply because it was my responsibility to do so…but I didn't. As an adult we tend to think differently. We know that there is a consequence for every choice we make however big or small. I am telling you that even in a bad situation you can choose to be grateful. I know that sounds a bit ridiculous to you right now, but just trust me. It's going to start to get less foggy as we work our way through this process. It may seem radical that events and situations that seem only negative can be changed simply by choice, but it is true. We live in a world…a culture that screams improvement. We are always looking for the next ring to grab. We have become seekers of betterment and somehow we have forgotten or not noticed the most important part of the journey. Yes, we are on a journey. Along the way there are bumps, boulders, barb wired fences and negative people. I am sure that if you checked your life experiences you could find something to whine about. But what good does that do? Your journey is also filled with opportunities and choices that are vital to your present and essential to your future. Have you not noticed them? They are the positive things or people that make you happy. They turn bad things into good. They remind you of what is really important. They are the challenges that make you stronger. They are those limitations that give you the opportunity to improve. They are the mistakes that teach you valuable lessons. They are the difficult times that help you grow. These are the places where gratitude lives and thrives. When we start to view our journey with possibilities gratitude can't help be show up!

Situations and Events

We all have them. Stuff happens! It is truly how you handle your stuff that makes the difference. Let me tell you that I too have stuff! It's always been there and it probably will always be there. That's a relief for me because I don't have to place all my energy in trying to get rid of my stuff. Stop fighting to clean house when you probably just need to organize your stuff. It doesn't matter if the glass is half empty or half full. Gratitude shows up when you realize that you have a glass and that there is something in it! I bet if you were asked to name some of the bad things or hard times you've encountered on your journey you'd be able to knock out a list in a snap! Think about that for a minute. Okay, now I am going to ask you to think about all those wonderful things and people you have come across on your journey. Think about what made your encounter with them so wonderful. Are you having difficulty coming up with as many good things as not so good things? Don't worry, that's average. However, I have a feeling that you are not average. Average people wouldn't still be reading this book. You might have been average at some point in your life but, something has changed. That change is the seed of gratitude planted within your heart, deep in its very core wanting to thrive. It's always been there. Some call it grace or the spirit that we all received because of the sacrifice Jesus made for us on the cross. I have also heard it referred to as instinct or intuition. No matter what name you choose to give it, we all have it. The need to have a better us, life and environment is strong. You might wonder why you've not heard its gentle whispers before. Perhaps, you were not ready to hear them. Fear of stepping out of our comfort zone will make you stay put. We like what's familiar. The unknown can be scary if you don't have a guide. Oh, but you have a guide! Y'all have not been introduced? Have you ever found yourself at a crossroad? Now this could be work related or life event. At any rate, were you not sure which direction you should embark? Did you hear a little voice trying to help you make the decision? Did you listen or decide to just fake it? Whatever you did…know this. That little voice may have actually been your guide. If you aren't used to listening to it, the tone would probably not be audible but you'd feel something. Did you feel something? That my friend is what a guide does, help you to make good choices. A seed planted if not fertilized will not grow. Okay, you knew that anyway, right? If you have never heard that voice inside you or felt that overwhelming feeling to make a certain decision at your crossroad …then your seed is dormant. However, you are blessed! The seed Jesus planted inside of all of us is an exceptional seed of the highest perfection. You can still activate it and I am going to show you how.

The Seed

In order to help you understand the seed I must first tell you a story. My mother was a complicated, interesting, determined, strong and a loving mother. She made mistakes, but what mother hasn't? We grew up poor, but we didn't know it. Our mother always made certain we had plenty to eat, clean (starched) clothing to wear and a comfortable home in which to live. My parents both worked. Mom as a housekeeper for a family over the mountain and Dad worked for U.S. Steel in the blast furnace. My mother was a professional stretcher of little sums of money. She wasn't a cookie baking kind of mom. I don't really remember seeing her smile much back then. When you live in survival mode you just don't have a lot of time for the extras. Times were difficult for my parents, but they made it look easy. Even when we only got one toy for Christmas, they made us feel like we had the key to the toy store. Most times, our gifts were handmade by our parents. It wasn't until I started school, that I realized everyone didn't live the way we did. Kids can be cruel sometimes, and my school days were filled with cruelty exhibited towards me by classmates because I was different. I have always loved books and going to the library was my favorite place to be. There I found an unlimited selection of books that had the power to take me on amazing trips. Library was my sanctuary. Within those walls were peace, joy, fun, adventure and no cruelty. I could be me or I could mentally transcend into places I wanted to go or assume a role that was powerful, daring and amazing. I grew up in the library and in those many books I read, I found friends. I could have allowed my classmates to ruin my perception of possibilities for my life, but I didn't. I could have felt sorry for myself…poor little girl who doesn't have the things her classmates deemed important in order to be somebody. I could have pulled myself deep within and simply disengaged with the world. I could have been depressed and allowed the cruelty to change me into someone who whines about her situation. At the time, I had no idea about the seed that was planted inside my core. I had already begun to hear the gentle whispers guiding me on my journey, helping me make choices. I didn't know what it was. I just knew I wasn't going to let anyone bring me down. I went on to attend college and receive several degrees. After my father's passing I convinced my mom to come live with me. At the time we were living in Virginia and I was working for the Department of the Army. My mom had not been well. As a matter fact, she had suffered several strokes and her personality had changed from the determined, strong and difficult mom I grew up knowing to a soft spoken, gentle and happy woman. She smiled all the time. Who knew that my mother told jokes? I certainly didn't. Now, they weren't necessarily funny, but we laughed almost has hard as she did while trying to tell them. When my mother died a couple years later, I gave her eulogy. It wasn't my idea. She had asked me earlier during one of our many conversations. I really didn't think I could do it and I told her that. She looked at me with that awesome smile of hers and told me, "If you really can't do it I understand. But, no one else is to give my eulogy. No one knows me better than you". I didn't take it as if she were pressuring me, because I knew she wasn't. But at that moment, when I said I will do it, it was because I heard that gentle whisper again guiding me to say yes. Instinctively, I listened and followed this guidance again. Something amazing happened on the day of my mother's funeral. Although I had written down everything I wanted to say and had taken those pages with me to the podium…I didn't need them. As I looked out on the audience and then down at my mother's face lying there as if she were merely sleeping it became clear. The whisper was no longer a gentle urging guiding me. It was now a voice audible to me as if someone stood beside me at that podium. I felt this vibration deep inside my core. It seemed to be slowly moving up from the depths of my heart. Slowly the vibration became words and I spoke them calmly and assuredly. Everything I knew about my mother came from that place and I never looked at my notes. Something else was happening. I knew that God had stepped up on that podium with me and ignited that seed within with the power only He could give. I was living gratitude. I spoke about all the things my mother had taught me and even though her death was painful for me, I felt so grateful! I was grateful to have had a mother. I was grateful to have had the time to get to know her. I was grateful that my children knew how much she loved them. I was grateful that my mother was no longer suffering the effects of all those strokes. I was grateful that I was her daughter. Lord! I was just abundantly grateful! Through my tears I felt the joy that surpasses all understanding. I have told you this story, because I want you to know that your seed is powerful…more powerful than you can imagine. It can fill you up with possibilities. I had been practicing gratitude all my life and hadn't given it a single thought. It was through my mother's death that I became ultimately aware that there was something inside of me that was spiritual and had guided me through some of my most difficult challenges. Understanding its origin and purpose was now vital to me. I had to know more….

Excavation

Have you ever gone on a dig? I mean like a historical excavation? I have always wanted to be part of a scientific or historical dig that revealed aspects of the past. The past…actually history has always intrigued me. To uncover evidence of struggle, wars, famine and great exploration would simply be an awesome job! I know, my historical nerd is showing. But I can't help but wonder about the events of the past and learn how these events molded our present. Much of what we do and know comes directly from that type of research. Someone simply decided to dig into the earth and minds of our elders and take a look inside. If you are feeling empty from all of life's challenges, then it is time to dig deeper for the good. I must warn you. This process might just get a little muddy and messy, but I think you are ready for it. You know yourself better than anyone, so I am going to ask a few questions and I would like for you to pause and give them some serious thought. But first, let's set some ground rules for this excavation. You're going to want to grab a note pad and pencil to write them down. There will be other things I need you to jot down later as we move through this excavation process.

Ground Rules

1. This is not about making the pain pretty. You have to feel the situations that occur both physically and mentally in order to move through them and acquire the positive.
2. It's okay to feel uncomfortable but please be honest. No one is going to see this but you. We are perhaps digging in an area that has been covered for years.
3. It's okay to be angry, furious or feel weak during this process. Digging is hard work but it has to be done with specific precision so as not to destroy the specimen.
4. It's okay to take breaks. So long as you are willing to complete the dig, rest whenever you need it.

Okay…let's begin. Because this is a delicate and precise excavation, let's start with the surface examination. When you look at yourself…examining the surface (Face)…what is the first thing you see? Are you seeing someone who you recognize? Are you noticing a smile or a slight frown? Does your face appear friendly and approachable or does it scream keep your distance? Maybe it just looks curious. That's perfectly okay. A little curiosity is a good thing. We all have a tendency to wear our thoughts and feelings about ourselves on our faces…the surface. Some of us block that surface with masks that lead others to think we are who we are not. Are you wearing a mask? The real problem with masks is that different people see us differently leading us to need more than one mask. Can you imagine wearing more than one mask at a time? Well, I did. I know all about masks. If you recall from a previous chapter I told you that my guide would whisper softly to me. That voice for years was never louder than a whisper. I heard it tell me many things that I simply ignored. It tried to help me make good choices but I brushed it off and dived head first into a mess! Depending on how many masks you actually have will determine how long it will take for you to discard them. Taking off a mask leaves you vulnerable, but if you are never vulnerable you miss out on life's endless opportunities for you to grow.

Okay...have you thought about those questions I asked? If you think you need more time to consider them...take the time. This is your journey and we all walk it at different paces. When you are ready...make some notes about what you find on the surface and keep it close by as you continue this excavation process. Don't forget the ground rules. They are your safe zone to assure you that you are digging well and that you're digging exactly where you need to be.

Now, as we move deeper in this excavation I want you to look over those notes you made again. Based on those answers, can you look past all that stuff you only let others see? Can you see the person that no one sees? I believe we are the product of our thoughts. Think for a moment about your situations. Our lives are compiled of countless ones. Specifically, I want you to think of those situations that may have caused you:

Fear
Anxiety
Stress
Worry
Pain
Disgust
Shame
Embarrassment
Abandon

You don't have to address them all, simply select three that stand out and you can relate a situation to it. On your notepad, write about the situation for each one selected, as much as you can remember. Try to recall when the feeling you've selected manifested. Once you are done, review what you have written.

Now, I would like you to write <u>one</u> positive thing that arose from your selected situations. I know this will be difficult, but please give it a try. Before you start, let me share my list with you.

<u>Pain</u>: When I was younger, I ran track. I actually was very good at it. Running activated my endorphins (didn't even know about them) and provided an overwhelming feeling of positive possibilities. When I was older, I was diagnosed with fibromyalgia. Fibromyalgia is a disorder characterized by widespread musculoskeletal pain accompanied by fatigue, sleep, memory and mood issues. Needless to say, running was no longer an option for me. However, having fibromyalgia has made me more aware of my surroundings and the people who occupy them. I have lost some of my physical energy but I have gained a determined drive to move forward. I still have my life and I choose to live it as fully as possible. I like to say, "I have Fibromyalgia but it doesn't have me!"

Embarrassment: I am currently retired. Before retiring I had a fast paced occupation that held a degree of importance and criticality. I balanced many projects and was awarded for my exemplary achievements by General Officers and Division Chiefs. I was a subject matter expert and loved every minute of it. Without notice I experience a stroke. It came on suddenly and paralyzed my right side. I was unable to speak or move freely on my own for several days. It was like I wasn't really me anymore. My recovery began quickly after a few days and to all outward appearances, I looked fully recovered. I was not. I found myself so stressed trying to recall tasks that before the stroke I could have done in my sleep. My job had not changed, but I had. I was so embarrassed because they had no way of knowing that the woman they once knew was gone! When the opportunity presented itself I decided to take advantage of early retirement. I was embarrassed that I could no longer function in that exemplary style I had gotten used to, but I knew I had to tell my boss the truth. I am glad I told her and grateful for this situation. Why? All my life I had been working at 100 miles per hour, excelling beyond many others but at that speed you tend to miss some really important happenings. I began noticing flowers, children laughing and playing in the park, the singing of birds in the trees and mostly I started paying more attention to that guiding voice that said, "It's time to retire." The stroke slowed me down so that I could see and enjoy my world around me and the people I held dearest to me…my husband and family. I am truly grateful that I didn't miss it all.

Fear: My fear is related to the situation above. Even though my guiding voice told me it was time to retire, I was fearful. My salary was extremely comfortable and retirement would only be a percentage. How was I going to pay bills? Funny thing about fear is it is not real! Oh, we think it is and if we give it our power it will make decisions for us. I remember sitting down thinking about my situation and I spoke a question into the universe. "How will I support myself when I retire?" You know what I heard from my guiding voice? My guide said, "Use Your Gifts!" Three little words that have opened my heart and fully ignited my seed of gratitude because when I heard the voice, it was no longer a whisper it was LOUD! I have no regrets about retiring. I am not rich, but all my needs and the needs of my family are being met.

Now, go get started on your list. Work through it at your pace. Remember, excavations are precise and delicate. I bet that once done, you will be feeling something different about your perceptions. In the next chapter, we will discuss that feeling.

More Than a Feeling

A feeling is defined as one of the basic physical senses; generalized body consciousness; to be conscience of an inward impression. (Merriam Webster Collegiate Dictionary) That all sounds well enough, but that feeling you have right now as a result of our excavation is actually more than just a feeling. Something has changed. When it happened to me I wasn't sure if I could put my finger on what it was. I just knew it had happened. With everything that challenges us in life, our mental default forces us to look at things negatively and believe the absolute worse. What is mental default? Well, let's break in down. Mental of course has to do with the mind, our thoughts and things that affect our conscience and subconscious perceptions. Default is anything preset by circumstances or situations that react on an automated basis. So, mental default would be those perceptions that you have already accepted that react automatically without little or no effort on your part. Let's look at this further. In a real life situation, our culture in which we live and grow molds us in many ways. Media plays a part in this because it is through media that we gather most of these assumptions that make up our mental default. Have you watched the news? I'm sure you have, but have you counted to see how many negative stories are reported versus positive ones? Magazines and movies are also participants in molding our mental default. Some people are simply just negative. They see only things to whine or complain about. If we surround ourselves with people like this, we start to see only the negative situations and lose our ability to rationalize the situation, shine light on it and find good. Now, I am not saying that there is anything good about violence of any kind. I am only challenging you to consider what good thing you can take away from the situation to make things better. We also see mental default functioning in our work environment. Some employers only notice what fails and address those elements because they have been molded by culture to fix what is wrong. That's perfectly fine, but you need to have a healthy balance. When excellence is ignored or not applauded and the squeaky wheel gets all the oil the rhythm of gratitude is off. Gratitude comes with its own healthy balance package. Included in this package is satisfaction, optimism, happiness, appreciation, ethical behavior, understanding, focus, motivation, selflessness, kindness, recognition, acknowledgement, respect, regard, assurance and the list goes on and on. When you think about the feeling you received when you completed your excavation did it conjure up any of the healthy balance tags above?   It did for me. The excavation can continue with you digging even deeper that you already have. Remember fear will creep in…but it is not real. 2 Timothy 1:7 tells us that God has not given us a spirit of fear, but of power and love and discipline. So push right through your fear and continue to take those situations from your mental default area to the reboot area. You have the choice to make every negative situation birth something positive. This is the nature of gratitude in action. Remember your journey has many situations and countless people. We can't hide from them. We just need to learn how to address them, organize the stuff and keep moving.

Fine Tuning Your Circuitry

Let's start by examining the path dwellers. Path dwellers are those people who live along your path as you proceed through your life journey. Some are nomadic dwellers who follow you around every corner and across every bridge. They are there for both the good and the bad situations. You tend to listen to them because wherever you are, so are they. Others are simply stationary dwellers who have built houses and planted gardens and erected fences because they have no intention of moving from their present place. These dwellers come in a myriad of personalities, sizes and demeanors. Some are meaningful caring dwellers who offer sound advice and genuinely attempt to guide you in the way they feel you should go. However, some dwellers are simply not as genuine and are not looking out for your best interests. My grandmother was a pretty wise woman. She grew up during the great depression and her view of the world was defined by it. Her family had a small farm with a few cows and chickens. They literally grew or raised everything they ate. Everyone rose before the sun came up and begin the tedious work of running a farm. I used to listen to her tell us stories about those days. She even showed us photographs she kept in an old hat box on the shelf in her closet. My grandmother was one of my more prolific path dwellers. Before I knew her true value, she encouraged my steps along my journey. Education was the key she said, that unlocked every door. There are many forms of education. My grandmother never went to school, but she knew how to read and boy did she read! Gram, as I called her, had closets filled with books. Late nights were spent mostly sitting on the floor at her feet listening to her read to us or reading to her from one of her many books. There were books whose names I struggled to pronounce and Gram would say, "Once you conquer the pronunciation of a word it belongs to you." My Gram was a stationary path dweller because she never moved from that farm but her words I carry with every step I make on my journey. Sometimes, stationary doesn't have to be a good thing. Sometimes these types of dwellers pass on their discouraging words trying to divert you from your path. Success is not what they want for you because they don't see it for themselves. They do not see themselves moving from their place on the path. Perhaps it is fear that keeps them there. I am sure you have heard that misery loves company. I grew up with a cousin who didn't place as much importance on education as I had learned to do. She always questioned why I was such a "bookworm" and a "goody-two-shoe" as she called it. She thought my wanting more for myself was my way of diminishing her as a person. She had long since stopped dreaming and saw no value in it for me. I believe that she loved me and was trying to guide me away from what she felt was inevitable disappointment. She figured that her life was only going so far, surely not as far as I dreamed for me. She said people like us don't live in pretty houses or go to college. She also said that school doesn't teach you how to survive only the streets can do that.   I love my cousin, but I didn't listen to her. Family can be pretty nomadic in that they follow you around either literally as you travel your path or mentally dropping their mental default programming along your path to virally infect your way of thinking. They often mean well, but they can only guide from where they are. If the dweller has never experienced anything more than negative, that's what they offer. Problem with that is it's not helping them and it won't help you. It isn't impossible to shake off the negative, but you have to first call a thing what it is before you can do anything to change it. Truth is, whether your path dweller is stationary or nomadic they can influence you and your walk in different ways. How do you discern which is good for you? You have to first conjure up the thought …is there more to this and then allow the voice deep inside where your seed of gratitude lies dormant to whisper…Absolutely! Once your circuitry is fine-tuned, you will know when the sound you hear affirming your movement is your inner guide or simply a path dweller.

Time to Get Real

Admit it. The paths we choose don't always take us where we want to go or ought to be. Sometimes we are attracted to a path because as we pass along it, we are touched by people, places and things. The people appear to be friendly, kind, intelligent. Houses look all cute and cozy. We decide this must be it! This is the place to be. We even build a house, plant flowers outside, erect a barbeque grill and invite friends to join us. But when the sun goes down, the path starts to look a little treacherous. The paint peels on the house, and pipes burst. The people become trifling and distant. The flowers die and the barbeque grill simply falls apart. Okay, this is the important part. What do you do now? Do you buy new flowers, build another grill, pretend the people aren't really trifling? Or do you check your GPS (God's Path-finding System) and ask God what to do? Can I share something with you? Life is rough, sometimes. The path is rocky, sometimes. People will let you down, sometimes. Your journey will not always be sunny days and flowers. It's going to storm sometimes. I believe I am God's child and so are you. We have been in the midst of warfare all our lives. The enemy, who I choose not to name here, has launched attacks from all sides using all types of people and situations. Why? It is because of the gift that was placed inside our heart by Jesus through His sacrifice. This battle will not be won by us, but we don't have to be casualties either. Pride is the enemy's gateway drug. Pride will lead you to believe you know it all. Pride will convince you that you don't need the gift Jesus gave you. Pride will lead you through the garden of denial into the direct path of doubt and fear. They will weaken you over time and make it easy for the enemy to work his play book on you. You will crash burn into the valley of despair, unhappiness and disillusionment. Your seed planted deep inside will remain dormant and you will not be free. Trust me, you do not belong there! Don't lose sight of the good things you've collected along the paths you've taken. Even bad situations present a positive possibility when you choose to collect a power motivating lesson instead of letting the situation stop you in your tracks. No place does it say life will be easy. Stop acting surprised when the path you chose changes and stuff happens. Remember, the choices YOU make are the ones YOU live with. The journey is rough enough. You don't have to venture down to the rock quarry and buy boulders to toss in your path. You have enough stuff already there. It is time to organize your stuff. Are you still reading? I'm just checking.

You Got Stuff

You might think it best to rent a dump truck and simply get rid of all your stuff. That would be a mistake. Stuff whether good or bad is ours to keep. It carries equal value in that it has the propensity to teach an important life lesson. Never deny or destroy your stuff. However, holding on to stuff stops being a good thing if you never review and organize it. Stuff happens continually throughout our life journey. Some stuff simply happens to us whereas sometimes we bring on stuff! The stuff that happens to us is usually beyond our control such as the death of a friend or family member, the attacks of 9-11, the tsunami. Although stuff like this isn't within our range of control, it doesn't mean we aren't affected by it. It is in the moment of the affect that we review it, and decide how we feel about it. Stuff as described above are horrific and emotionally devastating but they also have an element within that might surprise you. When a friend or family member dies we are of course saddened, but at the same time we are probably thinking how much we will miss them or how will we go on without them. Images of the moments you shared and the fun you had will eventually become part of your thought pattern and will, no doubt, become valuable. Here, right here is where the opportunity to organize and decide where this situation will be placed starts. Although it saddens you to lose them, your memories of having been a part of your life far outweigh the negative. These simple thoughts have poked your seed of gratitude and your inner guide tells you that person's life has been a motivating part of your existence. You have just encountered and achieved a gratitude moment. Gratitude moments provide clarity. They don't pretend that the pain of losing a love one is insignificant, but that you have decided to feel the pain and grow in spite of it to a place of being grateful to have had your love one in your life. On the other hand there is also stuff we bring upon ourselves. I was such a tom boy growing up. I was a daddy's girl and to me that meant if I wanted to be with my daddy I had better get used to touching worms. I would rise early on Saturday's to go fishing with my daddy. I helped him pack the truck and he taught me how to catch fish. I was pretty good at catching them, but when it came to cleaning them I always managed to hear momma calling. I did everything a boy would do and of course I thought I was better at it. I could spit further, jump further and climb a tree faster than any of my boy cousins. Momma didn't much mind some of my shenanigans but when it came to climbing trees she told me to stay on the ground! I bet you know where this is going. One summer afternoon, while momma and daddy were still at work, I climbed the tree in my backyard. I did it all the time. I liked sitting on the edge of the roof top and reading a book. Well, this one time I was so into this book I was reading that I didn't notice the car coming down the alley about to turn into our driveway. I was so startled I dropped my book and tried to get off that roof top before my parents saw me. Well that didn't happen. I grabbed for the tree limb and missed it and plummeted to the ground. I didn't get punished. Momma said my broken arm was punishment enough. She was right. I never climbed another tree, let alone sat on the roof top reading a book ever again. That stuff right there, I brought upon myself. My arm hurt like furious and I had a lot of time to think about my actions. It was a long time before I could look at a tree and not revisit that fall. I am grateful that my broken arm was fixed and that momma didn't punish me for being disobedient. We all got stuff. It's what we do with our stuff and what we choose to learn from it that matters the most. Now, this is what I want you to do. Still got that pencil and notepad handy? Think about some situations in your life. Divide them into two groups. One group for stuff that happens to you and the other for stuff you have bought upon yourself. Try to revisit each one. This time, rely on your inner guide and see if you are able to identify a positive motivating lesson that you can take forward. Decide if it is a growth lesson or one for the archives. Listen carefully for your inner guide's voice…pausing for a moment if needed. When you can conclude that the situations that caused your stuff to happen need not destroy you, you know you are on the right path. Remember, positive possibilities exist in all situations. Finding them will take practice.

Who took my Gratitude?

We now know what gratitude is. We've excavated the surface to identify the proper place to dig. Digging as deeply as we could, we have unearthed several key situations and events that we have encountered along our journey. Give yourself a pat on the back! Great job! Go on, have a celebration. You've earned it. Only, we are not done yet so don't party too hearty. I know it feels like we are, but we have to prepare for that moment when you turn around and it feels like your gratitude has vanished. Yes, that is going to happen. If you can recall, I mentioned earlier on that gratitude wasn't something you could check off your task list as done. I said it was a process that takes time. It will also need maintenance to keep it functioning smoothly as it travels with you on your journey. So, your gratitude isn't really gone. It's just been covered up by an event(s) or situation(s) that you haven't dealt with properly. We're human. Don't kick yourself for doing what any human being would do. You got comfortable and didn't realize the balance or the gratitude rhythm was changing. I think at this time, we ought to discuss a maintenance system. So, let's do that now. Imagine you have this tool box. Right now, your tool box is pretty much empty. You probably still have your pencil and notepad, but so much more is needed. I am going to provide you the tools you need to do your own maintenance so that you can tweak your gratitude whenever it starts to feel off balance. These tools are pretty powerful so make room for them in your tool box. By now, you should know I am not going to dangle gratitude in your face, let you feel it and not show you how to maintain it. Take a deep breath and let it out slowly. Let's get this tool box started.

TOOLBOX

(Gratitude Journal)

When I was growing up, I wasn't tuned into my gratitude as much as I am today. I didn't know how much it would help me, but my grandmother knew. I told you she was a wise woman. I spent my summers with her as a child. The farm was an amazing place for a child. After I had completed all my morning chores I was allowed to go adventuring. Gram's farm was a little over eighty acres, which seemed really huge to me. The town I lived in with my family was smaller than Gram's farm. Gram had horses and she taught me to ride. I always rode the same horse. His name was Hank. Don't ask! I didn't name him, but he was so cool. Of all the horses on the farm, Hank was the only one that followed me around like a puppy. He was beautiful! His golden coat shined like silk after a good brushing. I think he liked being groomed as much as I liked grooming him. Hank knew his way around and no matter how far out I rode, he always brought me back to the farm. One day before venturing out with Hank, Gram called me over and handed me a package. She had wrapped it in brown paper and placed a red bow on top. When I opened it I found a book inside. It was covered in fabric that had been hand stitched together. There were buttons, lace and ribbons attached. It was so pretty. Gram told me that her mom had given her one almost like this one when she was about my age, which was 7 years old. She had used it to write about special things that either interested her or happened in her life. She wrote about places she wanted to go and things she wanted to do. She also wrote about things that made her

happy. That day I rode Hank out into the meadows and sat underneath a big oak tree. I opened my book and finding a pencil inside I began to write. A gratitude journal is an excellent tool to place in your tool box. It only takes a few minutes out of your day, but it can bring you joy and strengthen your gratitude. You can write about big things or small things as long as you tune into the feelings of gratitude for having the experiences of the thing in your life. Go to a quiet place. Settle your breathing and concentrate on what you have been given in life. Have you been blessed with a great job that allows you to do that thing that's important to you? Do you have loyal and supportive friends and love ones? Do you have children? Are you and your family healthy? Are you blessed to be financially secure? Concentrate on what you have and not on what you want or are lacking.
Here are a few questions to consider:

1. What has brought me happiness today?
2. What has provided me comfort today?
3. Who or what has inspired me today?

The point to all this is to focus on what is giving you joy and peace one day at a time. A gratitude journal moves the positive front and center. Don't worry if your thoughts changes to something you are struggling with at the moment or on a negative emotional situation happening in your life. Don't avoid it, deal with it. It might not be obvious at the time, but there are always things to be grateful for in those situations if you take the time to really examine them. Look for something to be learned from these situations and you will soon be on your way to being grateful for them.

TOOL BOX

Gratitude Letter

In a controlled study, a group of college students were asked to think of someone in their life, past or present for whom they are grateful. They were then asked to write a letter expressing their gratitude and why. Once the letter was completed, the students were then asked to call the person and read the letter to them. They were all a little reluctant to actually follow through on this request, but they did. A few things happened as a result. Reading the letter to the person they had chosen brought gratitude into focus with clarity. Hearing the words as they read the letter reinforced their feeling of gratitude. The person they chose had a positive experience. They expressed gratitude to the student because they didn't realize they felt that way and it made them all feel pretty happy. Gratitude in action causes not only emotional joy but physical joy. Inside your heart softens to the kindness. It just feels great to know that someone is grateful for something you've done or simply for knowing you and having you in their life. Physically, it brings a smile to your face, perhaps even tears of joy to your eyes. Researchers have further discovered that when you think about someone or something that you truly appreciate and or grateful for that feeling triggers the calming autonomic nervous system. When this is practiced on a regular basis this simple trigger provides a protective effect on the heart. Practicing gratitude generates more positive emotions. This increase in positive emotions leads to a benefit in heart rate. Gratitude serves as a connector within the social emotions, awe, wonder, and elevation of good will. It not only makes the practitioner of gratitude feel awesome but the recipient feels great as well. It's a win win all the way around.

TOOL BOX

(Gratitude Living)

This tool is one of my favorites. As a girl growing up I remember playing outside all day long. This was before cell phones, internet and video games. No, there were no dinosaurs! Just kids having a grand old time playing in the park, kicking a ball around, swinging on the swings. We felt that staying inside was a punishment. Why would anyone want to do that? We used our imaginations to fill our days with adventure, excitement and fun. Take a walk in the park. Watch the children playing. Wait, on second thought, the park might be a little stressful however it will present the opportunity to practice finding positive possibilities in any situation including stressful ones. The park isn't doing it for you? Take a nature walk. As you walk, take everything in using all your senses and tag them with gratitude. Who can walk past a giant oak tree and not be grateful for the shade it provides. Within that tree, listen for the singing of the many birds that call it home. Look at the vivid colors of the flowers growing effortlessly without any prompting from us. They rely on the Father of the universe to supply every need they might have…and He does. There are many places where living with gratitude will improve your life and the lives of others. Nature is not your thing? No problem. There's always your workplace. The workplace is a challenging area to practice gratitude, but not impossible. No matter how tough and firm your boss might seem it is still important to show your gratitude. Don't forget that bosses often only hear problems, complaints, frustrations and annoyances. If the boss is having trouble balancing gratitude there is no wonder he or she seems tough and grumpy. Show your boss you appreciate his or her leadership. Show them you are grateful to have a job by doing the best job you can. Depending on your work environment, you might be okay just saying the words "thank you". Be careful not to overdo expressing your gratitude. You wouldn't want it to look like you're trying to win points or gain special favor. Remember, balance is important. If you are a boss, try telling your employees that they have done a great job. Who doesn't like to be appreciated for their efforts at work? If you are an entrepreneur you already know you need customers to be successful. How often do you tell them you are grateful for their patronage? There are several ways to accomplish this. Keep a file of your customer's birthdays and send them a birthday card each year. Offer discount coupons to return customers or have a customer appreciation day in which prizes might be won. The point is living gratefully means bringing gratitude along for the ride wherever you go. Whether it's the plumber who fixed your leaky toilet, the UPS person who walked down the driveway in the rain to deliver your package or the polite clerk who helped you to solve a problem, opportunities are always there for gratitude to show up! Gratitude has the power to turn someone's day from ordinary to extraordinary. I'm guessing you want extraordinary.

The Village People

We touched on the fact earlier that some people simply won't see the same vision you have for yourself. Let's be realistic, don't expect everyone to understand the new you…the one who understands and embraces the power of gratitude. Be honest, did you fully understand it before you started reading this book? I am certain that some of you were right there in the midst of gratitude and all it has to offer you…while some weren't quite as sure. You knew there had to be something more out there…but where and what? It's perfectly okay. One of my favorite quotes from the late Maya Angelou is, "I did then what I knew how to do. Now that I know better, I do better." We know better and we also understand the benefits. Keep your eyes open to your surroundings and those within it. No matter how awesome you feel from learning the process of finding gratitude in any situation you must be prepared for strange looks from the villagers. Your village consists of family, friends, coworkers, church members, the postman…pretty much everyone you come in contact with on your journey. As a child, I didn't make friends easily. I was definitely not the popular girl in any way. I was always interested in things the popular girls laughed and teased me about. I was a happy child and I truly got some strange looks from the kids at school. I discovered my gift of running pretty much after being chased by the mean girls every day in school. They thought it was fun to chase me across the creepy iron bridge that stood between school and my neighborhood. It was actually the only way to go if I intended to go to and from school. Having crossed the bridge many times, most people knew I hated it. It was huge, long and completely made out of steel extended above a murky creek. The worse part wasn't the fact that I could see through the steel openings in the floor of the bridge, but that on each end there was a portion without a rail. I imagined myself slipping on the gravel and falling into the creek every day. The ritual of the chase was frustrating, but I discovered that running across that bridge in fear of getting caught by the mean girls overrode my fear of slipping into the creek. They never caught me…but the thrill I got from running was powerful. I ran all the way home each day arriving sooner than the day before. I decided I loved running. Eventually they stopped chasing me, but I kept running. I am certain they thought I was crazy, but I didn't care. I tried out for the track team and was selected. I can't describe how happy I felt. I guess you could say I was grateful for the "mean girls" who chased after me daily. Were it not for them, I might not have found one of my everlasting passions…running. Don't ever allow the reactions from the villagers to deter you from using the tools of gratitude. Not everyone will get it. Not everyone will get you. That is okay.

Wisdom

Whenever I discover something great I always want to share with my family and friends. My girlfriends are always sharing awesome shopping coupons and sales advertisements with me. I love a great bargain, but more than that I love great information. Information increases knowledge. Knowledge can be communicated, but wisdom comes from doing the work and mindfully expecting to find something valuable because of it. For some people sharing information is a natural as breathing. Some of us including myself have to practice. When I think about information increasing knowledge and knowledge's potential to develop into wisdom I think of the disciple Paul in Philippians 4:4-7. It reads, "Rejoice in the Lord always. I will say it again: Rejoice! Let your gentleness be evident to all. The Lord is near. Do not be anxious about anything, but in everything, by prayer and petition, with gratefulness present your requests to God. And the peace that transcends all understanding will guard your hearts and your minds in Christ Jesus." This passage from Philippians reminds me that my thoughts affect my attitude and my mood. Have you ever taken inventory of your thoughts? Perhaps you should if you haven't done it before. Are you thinking thoughts that simply aren't true? If you are not careful your thoughts might lead you straight into the storm of problems. My mother always told me to think before you act. However, just thinking before you act is not enough. If you are not thinking things that are just, loving, kind or honorable it could lead to problems. Paul was informing the

Philippians how God instructs us to solve problems. When a problem arises, how do you address it? We are instructed to "pray with gratefulness in every situation". What does this mean? When your thoughts are not currently filled with the wisdom of gratefulness your prayers for a favorable response is ignored. God didn't say pray with complaining, whining, disrespect of others or entitlement. The scripture is clear. Don't expect a favorable response is you have not taken in the information, developed the knowledge and done the work to produce the wisdom needed to have a grateful heart. God promises that when you do these things, peace that transcends all understanding shall be yours. Not only will you be provided peace but that this understanding will garrison and mount guard over your hearts and minds in Christ Jesus. Now that's some wisdom right there!

It's All About Actions

Have you ever heard the phrase, actions speaks louder than words? The sentiment behind this phrase is expressed in many cultures. Historians think this phrase originated in English cultures in the 1700s. The book Will and Doom, written in 1692 by Gersham Bulkeley indicated actions were "more significant than words." It speaks volumes to the understanding of the connection that exists between behavior and character. When a person's actions contradict what they have spoken it injures their character and they become less believable and creditable. Also, when people ascribe to a certain belief system like religion that teaches humility and honesty but behave in reckless contradictory ways it projects an image of someone who doesn't live by their professed standards. When a parent tells a child it is a bad thing to smoke and that they should never smoke while the parent holds a lit cigarette between their fingers they are probably not convincing the child of the dangers of smoking. You get where I'm going with this? If you are going to share gratitude and encourage others of the power of gratitude, you need to be walking the walk. Nobody wants to hear you sprout your information unless by your very own actions there is clear evidence that the wisdom will be produced to grow and nurture gratitude. To be honest, your actions of gratitude will speak volumes about the benefits of gratitude. People are people watchers. If we were not there would be no need for tabloids. No one would care what Beyonce and Jay-Z was doing, wearing or where they were vacationing. No one would be interested in who is or isn't invited to the wedding of Kim and Kanye. Miley would just be this cute girl who sings great. Admit it, we are people watchers. I used to sit in the mall and watch people. Okay, honestly, the first time I did this, I was really tired from shopping and had all these shopping bags and my feet were screaming! No matter, I was sitting there watching the people as they passed. I watched moms interacting with their children. I saw a lot of men looking for a place to sit as the women entered store after store. I got a few strange looks from the guys. I think they hadn't seen many women actually sitting in the mall and not shopping. I saw couples arm in arm strolling and softly talking to each other. I also saw men dragging behind their wives or girlfriends. I couldn't help laughing at that. They all had the same look on their faces…"HELP!" So while you are out among the village practicing your gratitude, be mindful of the watchers. Your family and friends might even notice that something has changed about you, but they can't quite put their fingers on it. When they ask…and eventually they will ask, "What's going on with you?" Then pass along some information that might develop into knowledge and eventually produce the wisdom of gratitude. Let your actions speak for you.

The Heart

Whenever I think about my heart I am so in awe. Here is this amazing organ that is by far the most important muscle in the human body. It works as a pump moving life enriching blood around in our bodies nourishing every single cell. It has its own specific rhythm beating an average of 72 times per minute. A birth, the heart beats up to 130 times per minute. A woman's heart beats faster than a man. I am not sure why that is, but I read it someplace. If you wanted to calculate the approximate number of beats of your heart in a year…the solar year consists of 525,948 minutes and 48 seconds. A heart rate of 80 beats per minute would yield approximately 42,075,904 beats per year. Multiply that times your age and you'd have an idea of the number of beats of your heart so far. Yes, I am aware that sounded a bit nerdy, but interesting too, right? I mean, can you imagine anything working harder than your heart? In a more romantic view, the heart is the cradle of love. Our compassion and romantic emotions are said to be generated from the center of the heart. Here are some memorable phrases you may have heard regarding the heart.

- The heart that loves is always young. (Greek Proverb)
- The less you open your heart to others, the more your heart suffers. (Deepak Chopra)
- Smile, it is the key that fits the lock of everybody's heart. (Anthony D'Angelo)
- Only from the heart can you touch the sky. (Rumi)

- You can change your life by changing your heart. (Max Lucado)
- Let your heart guide you. It whispers, so listen carefully. (Author Unknown)
- The heart has reasons that reason cannot know. (Blaise Paschal)
- Love the heart that hurts you, but never hurt the heart that loves you. (Vipin Sharma)
- Nobody has ever measured, not even poets, how much the heart can hold. (Zelda Fitzgerald)
- There is no instinct like that of the heart. (Lord Byron)

I have to admit, I get a bit carried away when it comes to the heart. It makes perfect sense to me that the heart is where the seed of gratitude was first planted.

Sometimes when I close my eyes and try to envision it being placed by Jesus. What does the bible say about the heart? Proverbs 4:23 tells us that "Above all else, guard your heart, for it is the wellspring of life." Doesn't that command tell you that it is important to protect and nurture the heart? It is because the seed of gratitude lives there within the core of your being…the heart.

Life Flows

We now know that gratitude is a great thing. That deep down peaceful sense of appreciation and thankfulness we feel for people and situations in our lives is liberating and enriching. We don't just give our thanks and gratitude, but we have the capacity to connect with others and that affects profoundly who and how we are in the world. Gratitude makes our life flow in harmony with the universe, balancing the rhythm of everything around us. Gratitude creates more happiness and on a regular basis increases our feelings of wellbeing and contentment. Gratitude is a positive experience that reverses feelings of depression and despair. Expressing gratitude makes others feel appreciated. It increases the chance that we will see more of the qualities and attitudes in which we have expressed appreciation. Gratitude creates a shift in mindfulness. We tend to see what we are focused on. When we are stressed or over worked we tend to focus on the work that's not completed or the negative aspects of life. We are more apt to miss those tasks we have crossed off our list, the things we did well and the accomplishments we have made. The focus is on what we don't have and not on what we have. When you embrace gratitude you can create an atmosphere that leads to noticing and creating more gratifying experiences. Isn't this better than always seeing the glass half full? Don't stop at simply identifying what you are grateful for, lean into it. Spend more time with people who appreciate having you in their lives. Share your appreciation. Savor the qualities of your life filled with gratitude. Allow yourself to relish the situations, events and people that are compiled on your gratitude list. Keep adding to your list! Be present with your gratitude. It is one of the most life inspiring and exceptionally phenomenal gifts you can give yourself. I have opened the door to gratitude and invited it inside my life. If you are willing to do the work, embrace your seed of gratitude, something amazing will happen. Cultivate and nurture that seed and you will reap a harvest of emotional, physical and interpersonal benefits. Gratitude is a choice. Are you ready to make that choice?

Creating Your Gratitude List

A gratitude list is a simple exercise that will shift your thoughts to the abundance of your life. Spend a few minutes right now and think …what am I grateful for? If you get lost in the process…don't worry. Use the book as a reference guide. This simple exercise of making a gratitude list will attract more of the same good things into your life and nothing will be the same again. Enjoy the process and the journey.

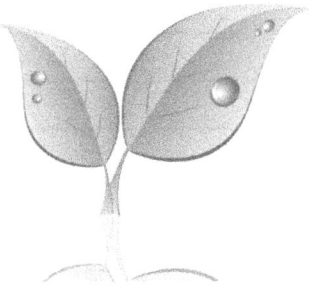

Your Gratitude List Awaits…

ALSO BY BEVERLY JONES-DURR

- 40 Day Joy Challenge, Finding Joy in Ordinary Places

- Naked in the Storm: A Wife's Desert Storm Story

Children Books

- Fairy Princess Training

- Trouble Makers

- Is This Your Elephant

- The Concert

- The Visitor

- Lonely Hoops

- Lisa's Amazing Bedtime Stories

- Lena's Secret Adventure

- Bennie's Garden

21 Day Gratitude Challenge

While writing this book, I created a Facebook group and named it Nurturing a Grateful Heart. I invited people to join the group and participate with me in a 21 day gratitude challenge in which I asked them to make at least one gratitude post each day for the duration of the challenge. The results were amazing. The following are a few postings collected during our 21 Day Gratitude Challenge. I have been empowered reading them and I know you will be as well. Enjoy!

Carol Durr

I started to write a simple post like, I am happy for this warm sunny Sunday. Then I remembered the intent of this Gratitude Challenge and now I'm going to tell you what I am truly grateful for. I am grateful that I woke up this morning and my son was in his room in his bed, not hurt, safe and secure. Thank you Lord!

Today I am grateful for being challenged in life. It's always good to be motivated and today I am just that, Motivated! I was asked to run the Tough Mudder (which is a 13 mile obstacle course in MUD)... and I'm going to do it!

Today I am grateful for my granddaughter. My son works nights and his wife goes to work during the day, so he watches her during the day, here at my house, since it's a bit bigger. I am blessed to be able to see her for 1 hour each day as she arrives at my house. On Monday, I took off the day and we hung out all day long. She likes to laugh and is always happy, unless you wake her up before she is ready, which I have a tendency to do. I am in love with her, and I am so grateful that she is in my life. It makes EVERYTHING ok! Awesome G-Baby!

Today I am grateful for the rain. I love the rain. It makes me feel calm. It helps me to know that I am not in charge and reminds me that there is something much greater than me working wonders in my life!

Today I am grateful for being able to go to the park, with my headphones on, and walk the entire park (4.5) miles with some running and take in the sights, sounds and smells of the whole thing. It was an awesome piece of peace and serenity. I Thank God for everything!

Years ago, at age 19, I married the man of my dreams. Soon thereafter, we had children 4.5 years apart. And now those boys are grown, that marriage has fallen to the way side and I usually home alone! While that may not sound so great to some, to me, it is everything! I am finally in a position where I can travel freely, I enjoy my granddaughter and I am so very happy! Today I am grateful for all the stupid decisions that lead me to who I am today! I love me some me! Thank you Lord!

Today I am grateful for having learned to be grateful... Sometimes, things go wrong and we wonder why did this has happened tToday I chose to think, why not me. The devil is busy and each time I get up, he tries to knock me back down. But, My God promised that "No weapon formed against me shall prosper". And I trust and believe that! So thank you Sweet Lord for the ability to be grateful in the eyes of adversity!

Melissa McRae

Today I am grateful for being able to spend a relaxing, quiet morning with my overworked husband.

I am grateful to God for giving me another day to enjoy His wondrous creations.

I am grateful that God perfectly loves, imperfect me. Not just myself of course but the imperfectness of all His children.

I am grateful for this day of rest, to relax, praise God, and reflect. Praise Him for another week, another day, another minute, and another breath

I am grateful for the sense of peace I have after time spent with my Father God, thanking Him for everything.

Today I am grateful for the love of being outdoors. Yes I could have complained that it was hot, & humid. Nope not me! My Dad always taught his girls the importance of when something needs to be done just do it, along with the fact that women can do anything men can. So while hobby worked on truck, this lady caulked all of the windows outside. I am grateful for all my Dad taught me growing up and grateful to my Father in heaven for giving me a fibro free day to enjoy working outside.

Reflecting back on the past 21 days of this challenge, I would have to say that I have always been a grateful child of God but I have not practiced gratefulness on a daily basis. Yes, every day I would thank Him for giving me another day, but often times I did not take the time to thank God for the little moments that I should have, even though I may haven grateful in my mind I did not verbalize it to God when I should have. I plan on continuing this more verbal and mindful practice of an attitude of gratitude. I am going to create a grateful page in my journal and make sure to at least write down one thing that I am grateful for each day. I am also going stay more in the moment and not let the small grateful blessings blindly pass me by. In other words, I think God is going to be hearing me say thank-you a lot more throughout my day. I have truly enjoyed spending the last 21 days being ever more mindful of gratitude moments, reading all of your posts, and getting to know about each of you. I do hope we all stay in touch as this beautiful time Beverly gave us comes to a close. I am always around with an ear and a prayer if you need one. I hope God rains down blessings upon each you and that you all stay my sisters blessed with the super power of gratitude.

Deborah Kienzle

I want to start the challenge with gratefulness to God for the journey of my life.

I am grateful to God for my children. The process of raising them has shaped my adult life. They bring out the best in me!

I've been contemplating today's gratefulness post since yesterday! All that kept coming to mind were the people in my life, past and present. I worried y'all would find that boring, uninteresting, and certainly lacking that uniqueness all writers and readers seek. Yet I cannot deny that the folks with whom I have had the honor of sharing life's ups and downs, triumphs and sorrows, are truly - second only to God - the source of my gratitude.

I am grateful for my memory. Grateful that I can recall the smell of biscuits and freshly churned butter filling my grandmother's kitchen, the sound of my father's voice softly - and sometimes not so softy - speaking my name, remember my middle age sons' childhoods with the clarity of yesterday, feel the sorrow of too many loved ones lost, yet still behold with amazing wonder the inspiring beauty that surrounds us all.

I am grateful for another quiet, peaceful day. Although I am tired this evening, I am amazed when I think just how strong we really must be, because each of us descends in an unbroken line all the way back to the beginning of time!

A Brief Summary of My Experience:

I truly enjoyed this challenge! I now realize I was probably born grateful. Appreciating and being thankful to God is as much a part of me as any component of my personality. Yet, writing daily examples of my gratefulness has made me think deeper and more often about those things. I plan to continue the practice. Much love to you all! May God continue to fill your lives with a bounty of glorious reasons to be grateful!

M. D. Taylor

I thought long and hard about what I would first want to share as the subject matter for my gratitude— do I speak about what's trending, while finding the gratitude in that? Or do I speak to something totally easy as the air blowing a sweet and comforting breeze?
Well, here's my first share! I am filled with gratitude to God, because I still have my Mother and Father here with me! There is no sweeter gratitude than to receive an unexpected phone call from my Mother~ she brightens my day because she believes in me no matter what—Trust me, when I say I have been given time to create great reasonable doubt at times for my parents. Also, when my world is off center, it's my Daddy who puts it back into place- he does so with that Fatherly advice and it comes so easily and makes so much sense that I can feel silly (especially at my age) for not having thought of the answer for myself— Oh, yes, the gratitude is in knowing that safety that only a parent gives to his/her child when they are in need no matter how old that child is and no matter the need. I have deep gratitude to God for gifting me the parents I have— all of them as I also have a step parent.

On this, my second day of participation, that of acknowledging daily gratitude, the following: Gratitude is defined by Merriam-Webster as "a feeling of appreciation or thanks." I am always thankful for each new day I am gifted continuing life. To be awakened by the Source of all life is indeed a sweet reward, especially when I think about the alternative to not being awakened eh--Today finds my mood grateful but somewhat blue because I am in the midst of struggle with one of my two (medical) chronic conditions— My struggle is that of pain today but though I endure pain, I remain grateful because I am able to have today off with pay. The former is such a simple amenity but there is great thankfulness in all of life's simplicities—at least for me there is. Time to heal without the worry of loss of pay is indeed reason for gratitude! I know that there are so many who are in need and want a job, a position, a place where they are able to earn their wages legally, while simultaneously earning the benefits of sick leave, insurance, and all of those little but important things we take for granted. Indeed thankful today!

Reference: 2 June 2014, taken from the World Wide Web
http://www.merriam-webster.com/dictionary/gratitude

Today has been filled with many a "honey due and/or do." Honey dues are just that-- daily tasks that must be paid for with the act of completion. For example, a few of today's honey dues required that of making payments to those things that are so much a part of our daily life yet we may seldom think (in any deep way) about the dues associated with them—like utilities, cell phone bills, groceries, and the likes. Sometimes a "honey do" is a simple request from a loved one, who says, "honey do" this or that so that we may have whatever end result we require that yields positive benefits for whatever is trending within our shared space and lives. For me those "honey do's" often entail running errands—can we say, yuck a couple of three times, while acknowledging the benefits associated with doing those do's? So, as I wind down for some much needed rest, I think now about what I am thankful for today—yep, you guessed it. This late evening finds me thankful that I have people in my life who require honey dues and more honey do's of me~ there is a certain joy that I find in serving others, especially those whom I love! How sweet the reward of their thanks to me with a smile, a hug, a sigh of relief in knowing or just that look, which says, "I love you for all that you do!" Yes, today was an awesome honey due- honey do day! I am giving gratitude to God for gifting me those who enrich the sum of my life.

I am a fan of the defunct sitcom called the "Golden Girls" and Rose Nylon is one of my favorite character's—whenever Rose is having a bad day she longs for a box of Velveeta Cheese and her bed—she said, " I want to crawl and hide underneath the covers and eat Velveeta Cheese right outta the box!" For Rose that is almost like buying a six pack of beer and downing each one. Today would have been a Velveeta Cheese day for me but for the saving grace bestowed upon me—In the midst of my storm today, I called out for help and it came quickly and right on time- I am thankful that I believe in God who gifts to me (unconditionally) all that I need. I know that not everyone here, on planet earth I mean, doing their little dance on the journey believes in God. Many believe that there is not anything or anyone higher than self and that self is what wills life—self is the only living thing which makes life happen. I am ok with others who believe in self only. However, why would you go Real Life 101 alone when there is something so much bigger than yourself, your ego, the sum of yourself and all of your life storms? For me that something is Father-Mother God. I am feeling favored, blessed and most certainly I am thankful to God for deliverance from a Velveeta cheese day! The greatest One is the creator and maker of all sentient life and I am a member created from that greatness with access to and through that Greatness! My brother's and sister's stretch the world over and we know each other by deed, by the way we speak and what a grateful tribe we are! Yes, today was one filled with the benefits of gratitude-

Everyday should be Sabbath if you are practicing the religion of Kindness~ Today I am thinking about the word and the deeds associated with kindness. If nothing else, it is so easy to be kind person vs an unkind one. I believe that when we live from a place not rooted in ego, that we are better able to enjoy all the gifts that are available to us for free like kindness, compassion, forgiveness, spirituality, love of self and others! So, today I am feeling abundantly thankful that I am aware, awake and choosing to love life and be happy with the sum of all gifts that fall freely from God daily! Enjoy your SUNday and be grateful to God for the gift of gratitude! Yay-rah!

Another brand new day; nonetheless, it feels touched by my life before—a kind of de'ja`Vu (if you will). Have you ever dissolved a long- time (say 25 years plus) friendship because of Real Life 101 circumstances? Often those circumstances involve life principles that are most important and fragile like trust, legality, truth, ethics, morals and etcetera. Today, I ran into a former friend who made an attempt to force me, to again, meet the new love in her life—still attempting to bully me in the same way she did when we dissolved our friendship. I felt sorry for her and then angry with myself for allowing her to "go there again." However, as quickly as my breath of sorrow for her and anger for myself did God restore me to peace. I am grateful to God for being present in those moments with me. Here's how: peace happened with quickness. Breathe deeply whispered God. Be still and know that I have removed this person from your life. You do not have to go and meet anyone. Simply share your known truth and I did saying, "you have introduced your love to me before and I do not desire to meet again that person. I am thankful that God has the power to protect us from those who no longer serve our best wellness, while simultaneously gifting us the ability to forgive those who harm us intentionally or unintentionally. Today really was/is a brand new day and I am inhaling and exhaling gratitude as gifted from God!

I was grateful for yesterday as well but missed sharing with you guys due to helping a friend get moved into my place- she finds herself, at this point in time compelled to get up and physically remove herself from her home and all that she has known. Because her environment was filled with "play" family, brothers and sisters, aunts and cousins (those are friends who are like family members but not related by DNA) and primarily drinking friends, as well as those actively participating in use of illicit drugs— she cried out for a safe place to stay—to live, to gather her bearings and to keep her new beginning. She had walked a path that entailed drug use and abuse before – as we say in my community, "she had been in that house" and she emerged, clean and back to wholeness. Sometimes a change of place and newly made friends is the best to beat down demons rooted in familiarity. So, I am grateful that God offers new beginnings to those who need them and it is, as I have said before, my pleasure to serve and help others. Sometimes helping others means just opening your home and heart, while trusting God to keep safe all that you dare to do for the sake of your brother, though he is for the most part a stranger—or in my case, your sister. I am thankful for the courage to attempt to be my brother's keeper.

Though late due to a family emergency today to include a visit to the ER (say yuck) all is well-- I just want to say, "thanks to each of you guys, especially Beverly for putting together such a wonderfuLL project for all~ the experience has been an enriching and helpful one-- at least to me! I have enjoyed it very much even though writing about my gratitude may have caught me short on posting-- I did write each day. I have enjoyed reading everyone's share and will have to find something constructive (hopefully equally as fun) to do in absence of posting daily-- I wish each of you a continuing and beautiful life and know that my gratitude is in having found each of you through this project-- loved every moment of hearing about you-n-yours (from grand-babies, to those military volunteers-n-soleful runners, to those struggling with chronic conditions and learning new languages, etc.). My life is forever changed for the better because of you, this group and its founder-- So rock on Sistah friends! If you want to stay connected by all means—

Taking time out of your busy life to just stop and look at your life may give you great cause for being thankful. Each New Year gifted to us brings about physical, mental and emotional changes- When we are young ones we cannot wait to be older ones! Do you remember saying in your best voice, with an affirmation and firmness, "I am 8 and half." Well when was the last time you heard someone say, out loud and proud,

"I am 49 and half years old." Oh, there is great cause to affirm our 49 and half years or whatever (your next number up the age ladder) but often times we do not make such statements. I dare say that if you do, you are that wonderful exception to the rule and a rarity too! I am an older one these days, past the age of wisdom! Nonetheless, I have days when I long for youthfulness and days when I am surely glad, I am not doing youthful (mainly foolish) things again. All of that leads me to today's share: I am grateful that with age there does come wisdom, emotional maturity and for sure one stops living from a place of ego mind especially where physical is the concern. Yes, we want to maintain our girly girl or boyish physical attractiveness—we continue to exercise and we eat healthier meals; however, we also do something that (for the many I suspect) we may have struggled with during those early years—that something is this: we learn to look at the sum of self and find the god/goddess within. In short, we learn at last how to like and love that face, that body, that winning personality! Oh, my goodness, we learn to love self just as we are (pause) . . . worthy to be loved as you have always been and shall be-Now, there is great gratitude in learning to love oneself completely—just as you are meant to be: perfectly perfect as you!

Simply gratefuLL for sunny Saturday Sabbath's! I hope your day has been filled w/gratitude too! Wow guys! Tomorrow is our last day to post for this project-- here we are already.

Today, I am feeling grateful for all gifts bestowed me! When I think about gifts bestowed I have to, on purpose, remember all of the little gifts that add up to offering me a comfortable life—am I proposing to be financially rich? Nope. However, I do feel rich in so many other ways- For example, there is a feeling of richness associated with those gifts that God has issued to me alone. Do you know what I mean? I mean those things that make you unique unto yourself; therefore, different than everyone else. Those character items that fit only you. For me those gifts are the most enriching! My gifts include the following:

(1) the ability to make others feel comfortable in my presence—almost instantly (2) a festive sense of humor (3) I am both a produced playwright and a published author of poetry. Therefore, today I am grateful to our Father for bestowing me with all those gifts that make me Emm Dee!

Thank you Universe- I am ready to receive all that you have in store for me in order to continue this process of growing (up) with God. Woot! Woot! What a journey it has been thus far.

Sharon Sanders

I'll start the challenge off by saying that I am so grateful for life. I have come to realize that life is not a right but a privilege from God. It's not because I am so deserving of this privilege, only that God saw fit, and through his grace and mercy, I've been granted the opportunity to live another day.

Today as I sat outside in the yard reading and watching my grandchildren riding their bikes, I thought to myself how it really is true. It's the simple things in life that can bring us the greatest pleasure. Therefore, on this day of nurturing a grateful heart, I am sincerely grateful for contentment.

With today being father's day, I'm so grateful that my sons are truly awesome fathers. They have loved their children unconditionally since the day each one came into the world. Not only providing financially, but most important, they are always there for them throughout every facet of their lives.

I am grateful for everything that I have. I don't live in a mansion, but I have a roof over my head. I don't drive the most expensive vehicle, doesn't matter to me one bit, because my only desire was to have a vehicle large enough to fit my grandchildren in. I'm by no means wealthy, however, I can say without a doubt that I am abundantly and exceedingly blessed.

Today, I'm ever so grateful that God continuously supplies all of my needs. Most often before I can even pray about it, he has already intercepted my thoughts and delivered it.

I am grateful today for having had the opportunity to celebrate another birthday with my granddaughter. I can remember that day nine years ago when she was born weighing all of 4lbs.

Lakennia McMiller-Dickey

Good Morning, (Nurturing a Grateful Heart) NGH Gang....very grateful to see another day!!

I am so very grateful for what I have. Life is so precious.

I am so grateful...my heart cries out, just thinking about His love for me.

I am very grateful that The Lord is fighting for me. "You will not have to do anything but stay calm. The Lord will do the fighting for you." (Exodus 14:14 ERV)

Today, I am so grateful, to our Lord and Savior. Last week was very hard for me...I'm a scleroderma patient, plus other illness. When the weather is bad, so is the scleroderma, for me. I have learned not to let this disease defeat me, Amen. I am so grateful to be in a good place today. Much love and have a bless day.

www.ingramcontent.com/pod-product-compliance
Lightning Source LLC
Chambersburg PA
CBHW081925170426
43200CB00014B/2836